Introduction

This booklet is the first in a series dealing with the techniques of feltmaking. It is intended to provide the information necessary for first steps in making felt but also to give an insight into the process to enable decisions to be made as to the type of felt suitable for the chosen purpose.

Felt has been defined as "a textile structure composed entirely of fibres physically interlocked and consolidated by the use of mechanical work, chemical action and moisture without the use of weaving, knitting, stitching, thermal bonding or adhesives". In layman's terms this means that wool fibres are felted by the application of heat, moisture and friction. This can be illustrated accidentally when washing a woollen sweater - if the water is too hot or the sweater is agitated too vigorously it will shrink and no amount of stretching will return it to its original size.

The craft of feltmaking is such an ancient one that there is no one way which could be described as being the correct way to make felt. Over its long history in different parts of the world variations of the basic process have been used. Modern feltmakers gradually develop their own techniques based on the old methods and on the essential factors which are required. i.e. moisture and friction with the addition of heat.

A single wool fibre viewed through a microscope shows that the surface is covered in overlapping scales. When the fibres are wetted with warm water and then rubbed they move and become tangled. The scales from adjacent fibres lock together, once this has happened it cannot be reversed and the longer the felting process continues the more entangled the fibres become and the firmer the felt. This process of felting converts wool into fabric without spinning or weaving.

Feltmaking is a very physical activity and requires the input of a fair amount of energy - nothing can be more demoralising than to expend time and effort in trying to produce felt and then to find that the results are not what you expected. An understanding of the fundamental process of felting is essential, careful study of techniques will give the confidence to make an informed choice of fibre depending on the required end result.

It is best for a newcomer to feltmaking to begin by making several small samples before launching into a large project. In this way knowledge is built up, especially if notes and records are kept of fibres, quantities and methods used. "Why samples?" - some of you will ask. The answer is that sampling is an invaluable way of preparing a body of reference material which will help to prevent disappointment and wasted time at a later date.

Wool Fibres

Wool fibres felt more easily than any other fibres and certain wool fibres felt more easily than others. Coarse wool fibres have large overlapping scales while finer wools have more scales but they are smaller in size. The size of the scales is also linked to the crimp (waviness) of the fibres. In general the more crimp present the smaller the scales and the finer the wool.

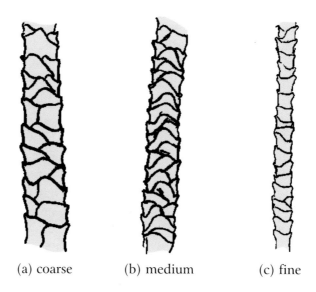

(a) coarse   (b) medium   (c) fine

Fibre thickness is a deciding factor of quality. There are two methods used to measure the thickness of wool fibres - one, the traditional count system developed in Bradford, is based on the number of skeins each consisting of 560 yards of worsted spun yarn which can be produced from 1lb of wool. The number of skeins becomes the count which ranges from 28 - 100. The higher the number of skeins the finer the quality of the wool. The other system of measurement used in New Zealand and Australia is the micron. One micron is one millionth of a metre. Fine fibres can measure as low as 17 microns while coarser ones can range up to 37 microns. An approximate comparison between the Bradford Count and microns is shown below.

Bradford Count	40/44s	56s	64s	80s
Microns	37	28	22	17

The different combinations of length, thickness and the presence or not of crimp affect the feltability of a particular fibre. As a general rule fine, crimpy fibres make fine felt suitable for garments while longer fibres make strong felt more suitable for rugs and for moulding into three dimensional pieces. With experience a feltmaker will learn to choose a fibre suitable for the planned end use of the felt.

Difference in wool fibre types

    1.   Long and coarse
    2.   Medium and wavy
    3.   Short and crimpy

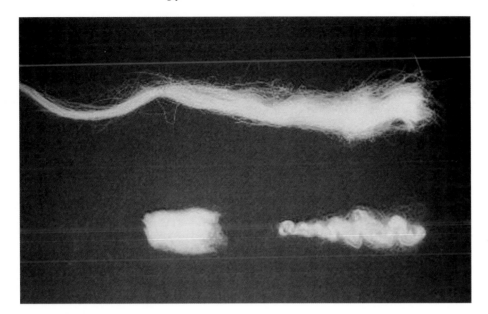

Choice of Fibres for Felting

The beginner feltmaker will find it easier to start with combed wool 'tops'. Tops are produced commercially from raw wool fibres and are part of the process of preparing wool for spinning into worsted yarn. The wool is first 'scoured' or washed to remove dirt and grease, dried and then put through a series of machines which gradually 'card' the fibres so that they are opened out and formed into a continuous rope of fibres. The rope is then combed to remove the short fibres. The long ones are left in the form of a thick but untwisted rope with the fibres lying parallel to each other - this is known as a 'top'. When choosing wool tops a good quality such as merino will guarantee good felting properties.

Using fleece for felting.

If raw fleece is used then it must be prepared by scouring to remove the grease and dirt. There are different methods of scouring fleece but a simple and effective one is to place the fleece in a net bag (the type used for root vegetables in a supermarket is useful) and scour in a series of buckets of water as follows :

    a)   Hand hot soapy water
    b)   Warm soapy water
    c)   Luke warm water with no soap
    d)   Cool water with no soap

Method

Immerse the fleece in net bag in bucket (a) and lift up and down in and out of the water several times. Empty bucket and gently squeeze water out of fleece. Repeat this process at each of the specified temperatures, then rinse in cool water until all soap is removed. Squeeze excess water out of fleece then spin dry (still in the net). Remove fleece from the net and spread out to dry.

The scoured and dried fleece should then be carded to open up the fibres. This may be done on hand carders or a drum carder.

Equipment for making felt

Old towels
Bamboo / matchstick mat
Bubble wrap plastic (small bubbles)
Length of heavy wooden dowelling or broom handle
Net
Plastic bottle with small holes drilled in the lid
Plastic jug
Waterproof apron
Rubber gloves
Plastic carrier bag - lightweight supermarket type.
Merino wool tops
Soap

Old towels

Old towels are required as a base to work on and to absorb any excess water. Contrary to general opinion it is not necessary to have the work place awash with water when making felt ! The towels should be placed on the table or worktop area to be used and folded so that they do not hang over the edge. This is important as if they do hang over they will act as a wick and the water will drip to the floor.

Bamboo mats

Bamboo mats are used to provide a textured surface on which to lay the wool fibres ready for felting. Bamboo mats are often intended to be blinds and are available in a variety of widths - the mat needs to be larger than the felt to be made. (Remove the blind fittings before using).

Bubble plastic

This can be used either as well as the bamboo mat or in place of it. Fibres wetted out on the plastic absorb and retain the water which reduces the quantity of water required. The bubbles on the plastic also add friction during the early felting stages.

Length of dowel

Length of dowel approximately 1 - 1.5 inches in diameter and should be longer than the measurements of the felt to be made. Broom handles are ideal and rolling pins can be used for small pieces. The dowel provides a rigid centre when rolling the fibres in the bamboo mat.

Net

Net should be larger than the felt to be made. Lightweight synthetic curtain net is ideal. A fairly open mesh should be chosen.

Plastic sprinkler bottle

1 litre plastic bottle with fine holes bored in the lid used add soapy water to the felt.

Plastic jug

Used to dissolve the soap jelly when making up the felting solution.

Plastic carrier bag

Folded into a pad it is used to press the water into the felt.

Apron and rubber gloves

For protection.

Soap

Pure unperfumed soap or soap flakes dissolved in water to break down the surface tension of the water and aid wetting out of the wool.

The process of feltmaking

Lay out the first layer of fibres with short lengths pulled from Merino tops

Place second layer of fibres at right angles to the first layer

Third layer of wool fibres in place with pre-felted shapes and fancy yarns as surface decoration.

Cover fibres with net, wet by sprinkling soap solution over the surface and rub with a pad made from plastic carrier bag until all layers of fibre are thoroughly wetted.

Remove net carefully after wetting out the fibres

Place wooden dowel on edge of bamboo mat and roll felt, bubble plastic and mat into a tight roll.

Roll the mat firmly with felt and plastic inside.

Completed felt.

To make a first sample of felt

Materials
Wool tops
Soap solution made by dissolving soap flakes in water. If soap flakes are not available then a bar of soap can be grated on a coarse grater and used in the same way.

Making up the Soap Solution
- Half fill the plastic jug with soap flakes then fill up jug with boiling water.
- Stir until soap is dissolved and pour into storage container to cool.
- To use for felting dissolve 1 dessertspoonful of soap jelly in hot water.
- Pour soap solution into the litre bottle and top up with cold water.
- This gives 1 litre of lukewarm soap solution ready for use.

Method
1. Lay out towel on flat firm surface. Make sure that towel does not hang down over the edge of work surface.

2. Place bamboo mat on the towel with bubble plastic on top (bubble side up) or if no mat is available lay the plastic directly on top of the towel.

3. Pull out small sections of white merino tops 3-4 inches in length and place in a line along one edge of the plastic.

4. Place a second line of fibre pieces on the plastic, half overlapping the first line like tiles on a roof. Continue in this way until the required size is reached.

Layer 1

Layer 2

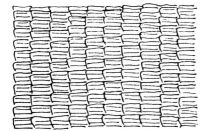
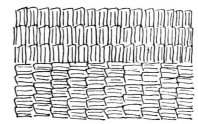

5. Lay a second layer of fibres on top of the first layer at right angles to it (see diagram)

6. Place a third layer of coloured fibres in position. Fibres in the top layer may be placed on at random and in whatever direction you wish to achieve the pattern required.(When preparing a series of samples it is useful to try a variety of methods on the top layer to find the different effects which are possible. (see notes on designing with colour).

7. Cover fibres carefully with the net, add soap solution by sprinkling from the bottle. Carefully press down fibres with the pad made from the plastic carrier bag and then using a circular motion gently rub the fibres with the net on top until they lie flat and are evenly wet through.

8. Remove net carefully avoiding disturbing the pattern

9. Place broom handle on edge of felt which is nearest to you and roll the felt, the bamboo mat and bubble plastic firmly around the broom handle. Next roll the end of the towel over the package to stop it from unrolling. Roll backwards and forwards on the work surface approximately 100 times pressing firmly down on the felt. Open up the roll, stretch out the felt to ensure that there are no creases, give it a quarter turn, re-roll and continue rolling 100 times. Remove the broom handle and roll only in the bubble plastic and mat for a third and fourth time for 100 rolls.

10. Test the felt to see if the fibres are hardened. To do this try to pick up a few fibres between finger and thumb - if hardening is complete the fibres will not lift from the surface. A second method for testing is to take hold of one corner of the felt and move it between thumb and fingers - there should be no movement between the layers of fibres.

11. If the felt does not pass the tests, remove the bubble plastic and continue rolling in the mat adding boiling water to the rolled up felt each time it is turned, pouring the water along the length of the roll - in this way the heat will be retained for longer. This process is known as milling - it compresses the fibres and produces a strong close felt.

12. Rinse thoroughly, spin dry and iron on both sides while still wet. Dry flat.

Shrinkage

All wool shrinks when it felts, some more than others and allowances must be made for this when laying out fibres for a project. Shrinkage may vary between 25 - 50 % of the original size depending on the fibre. If the finished size is crucial then it is essential to make a sample of the required thickness with the chosen fibre and to calculate the amount of shrinkage by measuring before and after felting. This would then be taken into account when laying out the final piece. But it must be remembered that feltmaking is not an exact science and that one of its joys is its tendency to unpredictability so there will always be a slight element of surprise in the final result!

Design in Felt

Coloured wools in feltmaking can be considered as the designer's palette. Just as a painter would choose the type of paint and method of application to achieve the effect required then the feltmaker must make similar choices with wool. A worthwhile exercise is to make a sample using coloured wools on a background of white - the white being the blank canvas and the coloured wools the palette. Look at a selection of postcards depicting works by different artists and analyse how they have applied the colour.

1. Coloured wools can be applied as areas of plain colour or they may be mixed in various ways. If a solid area of colour is required then the fibres would be overlapped and layered as described in the basic instructions

2. To achieve a gently blended effect the fibres must be mixed/blended before applying to the background. This may be done by hand or by mechanical means e.g. hand carders, small dog combs or a drum carder.

3. Changing the colours of layers of fibres will also have the effect of colour mixing as fibres merge during the felting process. The colours used in the layers will affect each other.

4. Areas of mixed colour can be achieved by finely chopping the fibres into pieces and applying them in small areas. In this way the colours remain clearly defined but the overall effect is of mixed colour.

5. If the design calls for areas of colour which indicate a specific direction e.g. horizontal effects then the fibres should be applied in the required direction. Wool fibres shrink back along their own length during the felting process therefore if laid horizontally they will shrink in this direction and this will show in the end result. The effect can be enhanced by the addition of silk or shiny synthetic fibres to the surface of the wool before felting as this will make the effect more pronounced.

Dyeing to Felt

Commercially dyed fibres can be blended to produce the hue or shade required, but if the feltmaker understands the basic principles of dyeing wool they can produce the range of colours they require for each project. Dyeing can be great fun, the anticipation of awaiting the results of a rainbow dyeing session is exciting but many people hesitate to 'have a go' because they are unsure of how to begin.

The safety aspect **is** important in all forms of dyeing and great care is required at all times. Some of the chemicals used can be harmful if used incorrectly therefore it is important to follow these basic SAFETY RULES:

1. Always wear rubber gloves and an overall or apron.

2. Protect the work surface with newspaper or polythene sheeting.

3. All utensils should be used exclusively for dyeing. All kitchen equipment should be cleared out of the way before commencing to work with dyes.

4. Avoid inhaling dust from dry dye powders. Wear a simple protective mask when using the dyes.

5. Avoid inhaling fumes from dye-pots - work in a well ventilated area.

6. All dye stuffs should be stored in sealed containers, clearly marked to show the contents and marked POISON or IRRITANT if relevant. They should be stored in a cool dry atmosphere and kept well out of the reach of children.

7. After dyeing is complete, wash down the surfaces which have been in use and carefully wash hands and fingernails.

Acid Dyes
Acid dyes are the dyes most commonly used for dyeing wool fibres. There are three types of acid dyes available but the type most often used is known as Acid Milling which is fast to both light and washing.

Rainbow Dyeing Wool Tops
This is a useful technique for dyeing fibres for felting. It is easy to do and produces a range of shades and colours from one dye bath which relate well to each other.

Choosing a dye bath
This should be a stainless steel container - a bowl, bucket or electric boiler (Burco type) depending on availability and quantity of fibre to be dyed.

How to begin

1. Coil the wool tops over the base of the container building up several layers until the container is three quarters full.

2. Carefully cover the fibres with lukewarm water with the addition a small quantity of washing up liquid and approximately 100 ml white vinegar. The detergent ensures that the fibres become thoroughly wetted out and the vinegar makes the water slightly acidic which is necessary for the acid dyes.

3. Press the fibres down until they are all submerged. The water level should just reach the top of the fibres. Pour off any excess so that no water lies above the level of the fibres.

4. Select the dyes to be used - one, two or three dyes per dye bath. A basic knowledge of primary and secondary colours can come in useful at this point. For example yellow + blue will produce green, yellow + red will produce orange and blue + magenta + purple will produce blue/red and red/purple etc. However it is easy to get carried away and add too many colours to the dye bath and the result will be disappointing muddy browns.

5. Sprinkle dye powders carefully over the surface of the fibres, avoiding breathing in the dust from the dye powder. Sprinkle different colours over different areas and allow the colours to partly overlap where they meet so that the colours will mingle. A little black dye powder may be sprinkled in small areas to dull bright colours.

6. Avoid the temptation to poke the fibres or the dyes as this will cause the dye powders to mix. Cover the dye bath with the lid of the container or aluminium foil. If using foil make two or three small holes with a knitting needle to allow steam to escape.

7. Raise the temperature of the dye bath slowly to simmering point. A small container should take approximately thirty minutes to reach simmering while a larger one should take forty-five minutes to an hour.

8. When the dye bath reaches simmering point, turn down the heat so that the temperature is just maintained for a further forty-five minutes. The dye bath must not be allowed to boil as the movement of the water will cause the wool tops to felt.

9. Switch off the heat and allow the dye bath to cool without touching the wool.

10. Rinse carefully in lukewarm water to remove any excess dye.

11. Wash gently in warm soapy water and then rinse carefully in warm water until water is clear.

12. Place the dyed tops in a net bag (the type used for onions and carrots) and spin dry.

13. Gently straighten tops and open them up slightly before drying.

When dry, the fibres can be used straight from the tops, or they can be blended further by lightly carding with hand carders or a drum carder. A little time spent preparing several dye baths can produce fibres in a wide colour range.

Another interesting experiment is to add some yarns or other fibres such as cotton, linen, silk etc. to the dye bath at the same time as the wool tops - this will produce different effects as the different fibres take up the dye in different ways. Acid milling dyes are primarily intended for protein fibres but vegetable fibres often take up some dye and may produce paler shades than the wool which would add another dimension to the felt.

Microwave Dyeing

For safety reasons this process should not be carried out in a microwave oven which is normally used for food. A microwave is a useful tool for quick and easy dyeing using acid milling dyes. The same method is suitable for both wool and silk fibres but is particularly successful with silk. For this method of dyeing the dye powder is made up into a solution and applied with plastic syringes. It is useful to make up the dye solution to a known strength so that it is easier to calculate the quantity of dye applied to the fibres.

Equipment

Scales which will weigh 1 gm - diet scales are useful or a measuring spoon as used for cooking
Plastic beakers marked in ml or measuring jug
Glass rod or similar for stirring solutions.

To make up a 1% dye solution :

1. Weigh 1 gm of dye powder and place in a 100 ml beaker

2. Add approximately 30 ml of hot water and stir with a glass rod until all the lumps are removed (just like making custard).

3. Carefully fill up the beaker to the 100 ml mark with boiling water and stir thoroughly.

4. Allow to cool and store until required in a carefully labelled container.

5. If a larger quantity of solution is required then increase the weight of dye powder and water in the exactly the same proportions eg 5 gms dye powder made up to 500 mls gives 500 mls of 1% dye solution.

Acid milling dyes have a long shelf life if stored in cool dark conditions so it is useful to make up larger quantities of dye and store until required but is essential to label the container carefully. See sample label.

> ## MAGENTA 1%
> ## ACID MILLING DYE
> ## DATE : 23/02/02

Rainbow Dyeing in a Microwave

1. Thoroughly wet out the fibres in lukewarm water with the addition of a few drops of detergent and 50 ml white vinegar to 1 litre of water. Silk is difficult to wet out and requires soaking for several hours.

2. Squeeze fibres from the soaking liquid and place in a layer in the base of a microwave proof container - the fibres should be wet but have no excess liquid lying around them.

3. Apply the dye solution with syringes. two or more colours may be used, overlapping the colours as previously described.

4. Press the dye down into the fibres - an old potato masher is useful for this or you can use your hands if protected with rubber gloves. Turn the fibres over and if necessary add more dye solution. The fibres should be coloured but there must be no loose dye solution in the base of the container.

5. A second layer of fibres may be added and dye applied in the same way.

6. Cover container with cling film and place in the microwave on full power for five minutes.

7. Repeat on half power for three / four minutes.

8. Allow fibres to cool then rinse thoroughly and allow to dry.

Further Techniques

If the design calls for clearly defined shape then the fibres must be prefelted into a sheet and then cut out as required before application to the background. In this way the shape is maintained throughout the felting process.

Pre-felt

The term pre-felt is used to describe a sheet of wool fibres which have been processed just enough to make them hold together but the treatment stopped before the fibres are felted.

How to make pre-felt:

1. Lay out two layers of fibres on bamboo mat/bubble wrap (see instructions for making felt) and cover with net.
2. Wet out fibres with soap solution
3. Rub gently with plastic bag to remove all air bubbles.
4. Gently remove the net
5. Roll firmly in the bamboo mat/bubble plastic with a dowel 100 times.
6. Open up the roll, quarter turn the sheet of fibres and reroll 100 times.
7. Test with fingers to see if they are holding together but not felting.
8. Rinse carefully and gently squeeze the water out.
9. Iron on both sides and leave to dry flat.

Inlay Technique

In this technique the shapes to be inlaid are cut out of prepared pre-felted pieces. The background batt of fibres is laid down in the usual way, covered with net, wetted out and rubbed lightly just enough to flatten the fibres. The net is then removed. The cut pieces of pre-felt which are to form the pattern are carefully laid on the surface of the background batt and pressed down so that they adhere to the wet fibres below. If it is crucial that the pattern pieces do not move at all then they should be lightly tacked in position with fairly large tacking stitches.

The net is then replaced and the inlaid pieces gently rubbed with soap to ensure that they are thoroughly wetted. the net is removed and the felting process continued. After two rollings with the dowel in place any tacking stitches should be carefully removed to prevent them becoming enmeshed in the felt.

As the fibres begin to felt the pre-felted shapes become an integral part of the main piece. A good way to test this is to make a sample with brightly coloured pre-felted pieces on a light coloured background. When the felting is complete the coloured outlines of the inlaid shapes are clearly visible on the underside of the felt, showing that the coloured fibres are thoroughly felted in with the background fibres and not just sitting on the surface.

Mosaic Technique

Another method of using pre-felt builds up a pattern by fitting pieces carefully together over the whole surface of the felt like a mosaic. Using this method the surface of the felt is completely level unlike the inlay technique where the inlaid pieces are slightly above the level of the background fibres.

To make a mosaic pattern two layers of different coloured pre-felt are put one on top of the other. A paper pattern is then pinned in position through both layers and the required shape carefully cut out. When cutting out the shapes the point of the scissors should be inserted as close as possible to the edge of the pattern so that the felt surrounding the pattern remains intact. If a dark and a light colour are used the dark shape cut from the dark felt can be inserted in the identical space left in the light felt and vice versa. To keep the pieces in place they should be lightly tacked with fairly long oversewing stitches. Once the mosaic pattern has been built up it should be placed on to a background batt of unfelted fibres and the whole package then felted together. When the fibres begin to hold together carefully remove the tacking stitches before completing the felting processes.

Pattern pinned in position

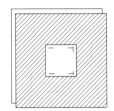

Mosaic built up from two colours of felt

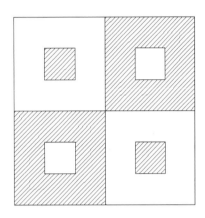

Weaving Pre-felt

A third way in which pre-felt can be used is to cut it into strips and weave it together to form a pattern. By using different colours, different interlacings and if wished, different widths of strips, interesting designs can be formed. Once the strips have been interwoven the piece should be tacked together around the edges to hold them in place and the whole piece laid onto a batt of unfelted fibres and felted together. Again the tacking stitches should be removed before they become enmeshed in the felt. If the piece being 'woven' is large then it is helpful to pin the top of each vertical strip down on to a piece of soft fibre board and then as each horizontal strip is woven in, it should be pushed up into position and each end pinned before tacking to hold it in place.

Pre-felt strips pinned in position

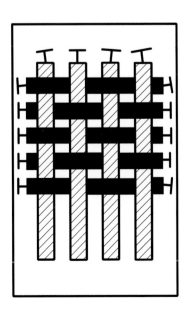

Multi-layered Felt

This is built up from layers of different coloured fibre and may be made from unfelted fibres, pre-felt or a mixture of both. This can be time consuming to make as it takes time for the felting process to take place in the inner layers but is very effective. Once completed, parts of the top layers can be cut away to reveal the colours underneath. If the felt is left fairly soft the edges spring back when cut which can be very suitable for purely decorative purposes. If the felt is well hardened and milled the edges remain firm after cutting.

Incorporating other Fibres, Yarns and Fabrics into Felt

Yarns and scraps of fabric can be added to the surface of the wool fibres before felting begins. This can produce interesting results. As the felting progresses, the wool fibres shrink, causing the yarns and fabric to wrinkle up and produce textured effects. Fibres with a hairy or textured surface e.g. mohair or boucle yarns, work well and fabrics with a slightly rough surface adhere better than fabrics which are too smooth. To help fabric adhere to the surface of the felt it is a good idea to fray out some threads around the edges of the pieces before placing them on the wool fibres - the short ends of the threads then become caught up in the fibres. Different effects can be obtained by laying the wool fibres on to a layer of fabric and felting both together. If the fabric is fairly loosely woven then this technique works particularly well. As the felting progresses some of the fibres make their way through the weave structure of the fabric and as the fibres shrink the material contracts producing a textured surface. The results achieved vary with the fabric used - cotton muslins and scrims work well giving a fine texture on the reverse of the felt while synthetic chiffons produce a more textured bubbled effect. Open weave cottons can be first decorated by printing, painting or tie dyeing before laying on the wool fibres and as the felt shrinks so too does the pattern on the fabric and again interesting textures appear.

Using Fabric Paints and Crayons

Designs can be painted on the surface of the already made felt - this may be done using fabric paints or dye. Stencilling is a very satisfactory method of applying paint or dye as it is possible to work the colour well into the felt. Felt can be tie dyed after it is made or random dyed in a flat tray using dyes in powder form - it is best to follow the suppliers' instructions.

Patchwork

Patterns can be created by invisibly stitching small pieces of felt together - this is an ideal way in which to use up scraps left over from other projects.

Quilting

Hand or machine-stitching can be used to decorate and to reinforce felt especially if spirals or zig-zag lines are used. This technique of stitching on felt is apparent on many ethnic examples.

Embroidery

Embroidery is a very useful addition to the surface of felt. It may be done by hand or machine. Surface stitching adds interest as it creates contours and breaks up the otherwise flat surface of the felt.

Sunset - pictorial felt with blended colours in the background Pre-felted shapes give the hills a clear outline.

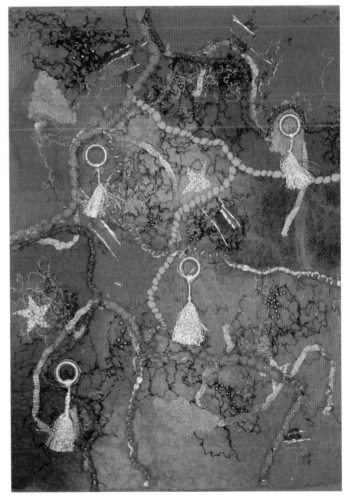

Tassels - silk threads felted into the background. Couched felted cords and metallic tassels add surface texture.

Pill box hat with piecrust edge - made from a flat piece of felt.

Rug hand-felted in Konya, Turkey under the tuition of feltmaster Mehmet Girgic. The traditional design uses naturally dyed pre-felted wool on a background of New Zealand cross-bred with Anatolian mountain wool.

Sample of inlay technique.

Edges

If the completed piece of felt is to be cut up and seamed then the edges can be ignored but if the finished edges are to be seen, as in the case of a decorative wall-hanging, then it is necessary to deal with them throughout the felting process. After the fibres have been wet out and rubbed to flatten there are several methods which can be employed.

1. fold under any straggling ends of fibre

2. trim the edges to the required shape

3. add an extra layer of fibre around the edges to prevent thinning and spreading.

After every rolling the edges should be checked and knocked back into shape or trimmed when necessary. This should be done in the early stages so that edges are set before felting is completed.

Conclusion

The information provided in this booklet guides the beginner feltmaker through the basic steps in making flat felt and offers many possibilities for producing individual designs within the felt.

Suppliers

Adelaide Walker
2 Mill Yard Workshops
Wharfedale Business Centre
Otley Mills
Ilkley Road
Otley LS21 3JP
Tel : 01943 850812
Good range of fibres

George Weil
Old Portsmouth Road
Peasmarsh
Guildford
Surrey
GU3 1LZ
Tel: 01483 565800
Fax: 01483 565807
Fibres, dyes, books, informative catalogue

Wingham Wool Work
70 Main Street
Wentworth
Rotherham
South Yorkshire
S62 7BR
Tel: 01226 742926
Fax: 01226 741166
Wide range of fibres and books

Kemtex Colours
Chorley Business & Technology Centre
Euxton Lane
Chorley
Lancashire
PR7 6TE
Tel: 01257 230220
Fax:01257 230225
Wide range of dyes, instruction booklets

Further Reading

Belgrave, Anne   How to Make Felt.
Search Press 1995 ISBN 0-85532-795-2

Burkett, M.E.   The Art of the Feltmaker.
Abbot Hall Art Gallery, Kendal, 1979 ISBN 0-9503335-1-4

Evers, Inge   Feltmaking Techniques and Projects.
Translated by Marianne Weigman. Lark Books, 1987
ISBN 0-7136-2950-9

McGavock, Deborah   Feltmaking The Crowood Press Ltd.
Lewis, Christine   ISBN 1861263082

Sjoberg, Gunilla Paetau   Felt - New Directions for an Ancient Craft.
Translated by P. Spark. Interweave Press, Inc., 1996.
ISBN 1-883010-17-9

Batt
The preparation stage for feltmaking. Webs of fibres are peeled off hand or drum carders and then layered to form a batt several centimetres in depth. Alternatively short lengths of fibres are pulled from combed tops and placed side by side to form a batt several layers deep.

Blending
A process in the preparation of wool fibres when different colours colours can be carded together for decorative effect. Also used for combining fibres of different characteristics, types or qualities.

Bradford Count
The measure of fineness of wool based on the number of hanks of yarn each 560 yards in length which can be worsted spun from one pound weight of wool fibres e.g. if 50 hanks are spun the count is then 50s.

Breeds
The generic term used in the classification of sheep which is then sub-divided according to type :- Shortwool and Down, Medium, Longwool and Lustre, Mountain and Hill.

Carding
The process of teasing and opening out wool to separate the individual fibres. The result of hand or drum carding is a lap of aligned fibres in preparation for spinning or feltmaking.

Combing
A process after carding which is for the preparation of worsted yarn. The worsted yarn. The combing process removes the shorter fibres (Noil) leaving the longer fibres to produce a smoother yarn when spun. *(see Worsted)*.

Count
As for Bradford Count. Also known as Bradford Quality Numbers.

Crimp
The visual waviness of wool fibres. Crimp varies greatly according to wool quality. It can be measured as crimps per centimetre.

Felt
A generic name given to a fabric where wool fibres are interlocked and entangled. With the application of moisture, heat and friction they are transformed into a compact mass and become felt.

Fibre(s)
Individual hairs which are grown collectively as fleece on sheep. Other animals such as alpaca, camel and cashmere, produce hair fibres. Fibres can be of vegetable origin e.g. cotton, or synthetic as in nylon. The varying length of the fibre is called the staple. *(See Staple)*

Fleece
The shorn wool of a sheep. It can mean the whole fleece or a mass of wool fibres.

Fulling
A process which compacts the felt and increases the density by using further friction and heat. *(See Milling)*.

Half - Felt
Also known as pre - felt. Fibres which have been cross layered and felted just enough to form a cohesive sheet but which have not begun to shrink. Used for inlay and mosaic techniques in felt design.

Hardening   The continuing process of felting from the pre-felt stage to the point where it is cohesive and has become a low density felt.

Inlay   A technique in felt design. Prefelted pieces are cut into shape and placed on a batt of unfelted fibre and the whole is then felted together. felted together.

Merino   A breed of sheep producing fine wool of 60s count upwards. It is of Spanish origin but thrives in Australia, South Africa and New Zealand.

Micron   A Measurement of fibre thickness. One micron equals one millionth of a metre. An alternative to the Bradford Count System. It is used mainly in the Southern Hemisphere.

Milling   The process after hardening which increases the density of felt. *(See Fulling).*

Mosaic   Design built up of pre-felted pieces fitted together to form an all over design. This layer may then be placed on an unfelted batt and the whole felted together - this produces a felt with a flat smooth surface.

Noil   Short wool fibres which are removed by combing. This is a necessary preparation for worsted spinning. Noil is very useful in feltmaking and can be Blended with other fibres

Pre-felt   Also known as half - felt. Fibres which have been cross layered and felted just enough to form a cohesive sheet but which have not begun to shrink. Used for inlay and mosaic techniques in felt design.

Quality   The quality of wool is expressed as a number. The higher numbers indicate finer wools, the lower ones coarser grades. Merino could be 60s plus but Herdwick 30s. Average qualities are 48s - 58s.

Scales   The distinctive feature of animal fibres which makes the fibre rough in one direction and smooth in the other. Having scales is the characteristic essential for the ability of wool to felt.

Scour   The process of removing dirt, grease, suint and vegetable matter from fleece by washing.

Staple   Generally the term given to the length of fibres but can mean a cluster of fibres also called 'locks'. Staples or locks are used when grading wool for length, texture and coarseness.

Tops   Commercially prepared fibres combed into long strips like a loose rope. The long fibres are parallel, well separated and are ideal for making lightweight felt of high quality.

Woollen   The process of spinning a yarn from both the long and short fibres of a fleece. The whole locks when carded, can be used for feltmaking without other preparation.

Worsted   The result of removing the short fibres when preparing a fleece. After carding the fibres are combed, leaving parallel, smoother fibres. *(See Carding, Noil, Woollen).*